Artful–Playful–Mindful in Action

Orff-Schulwerk Classroom Projects for a New Generation of Learners

Edited by Leonard Davis and Diana Hawley Larsen

with Foreword by Jane Frazee

T0078731

SMC 580

SMC 580

UPC 841886026070

ISMN M–60001–239–8

ISBN 978–1–84761–403–2

British Library Cataloguing-in-Publication Data.

A catalogue record for this book is available from the British Library

Design, typesetting and music engraving by William Holab

Contents

Foreword

This book's subject is the craft of music teaching. It is brought to life by the authentic stories of real teachers in real classrooms who have undertaken the adventure of introducing a new Orff-Schulwerk curriculum to their students—a curriculum that involves making, making up, and making sense of sound. The narratives attest to the effectiveness of a new kind of learning that involves student reflections on the music they have made together. This unique model, based on Orff-Schulwerk principles, insists that reflection on the doing is the path toward musical understanding.

Beyond craft, however, the art of music teaching is illustrated here. The teachers' observations suggest that as students attend to sounds, their responses grow and deepen. They are hearing and feeling what it is like to be a musician!

The teachers who have kindly shared their excitement and expertise in this Orff experiment are fourth generation American Orff practitioners. As Orff training programs have grown in rigor, these teachers have come to realize that their encounters with students must reach beyond simply participating in singing, saying, moving, and playing activities. Active involvement in these bedrocks of the Orff approach is viewed as the entrance to a broader understanding of music itself.

And—because every music teacher is committed to advocating for music's place in the educational enterprise—you'll find that the lessons in this book illustrate that learning about music is like learning about anything. Students concentrate, remember, invent, analyze, revise, and work collaboratively—all important contributions to mastering tasks inside and outside the music room.

Just as Orff classes are collaborative, so is this book a collective effort. The teachers began with the notion of field testing the *Artful–Playful–Mindful* theoretical model and then communicated what they learned with one another. Happily, they have now chosen to share some of their outcomes with you!

—JANE FRAZEE

Contributors

Karen K. Benson holds B.M. and M.M. degrees from the University of Nebraska-Lincoln. Currently in her 28th year of teaching, she instructs children in grades PreK-5th at William F. Cody Elementary, an All Title I learning community of the Millard Public Schools in Omaha, Nebraska. Focused on hard work and families, Cody is home to several unique programs including special needs and income based preschool classes, alternate curriculum classes, and the Orff-Schulwerk Honors Ensemble that Karen co-directs. She is a Past President of the American Orff-Schulwerk Association and represented AOSA at the 2011 Orff Symposium and the 2011-2012 meetings of The Orff Forum in Salzburg, Austria. She teaches AOSA Teacher Education Certification courses and serves as a workshop clinician at numerous professional development music conferences, school districts, and AOSA regional chapters.

Rachel Bergeron has been teaching music in public schools at the elementary and middle school levels for 18 years. She is currently the Music Specialist at Laurel School, a California Distinguished elementary school in Atherton, CA. She teaches 400 students in grades K-3 and directs two elementary school choruses. Rachel Bergeron graduated with a B.M. in Music Education from Marywood University, Scranton, PA. She received a M.A. in Music Education with a concentration in Orff-Schulwerk from the University of St. Thomas, Saint Paul, MN. Rachel presently serves as President of NCAOSA, and has been a member of the NCAOSA Board for almost 10 years. She attended the International Summer Course at the Orff Institute in Salzburg in 2005.

Leonard Davis has 12 years of music teaching experience in both private and public school systems. He currently teaches 500 students at Garfield-Challenge Center Elementary in Sioux Falls, South Dakota. Two public schools in the same building, Garfield serves a Title I community and the Challenge Center is a specialized school for gifted and talented learners. Lennie received his B.M. degree from Northern State University, Aberdeen, SD, and a M.A. in Music Education from the University of St. Thomas, St. Paul, MN. He has completed all levels of Kodály and Orff-Schulwerk Teacher Education, and is the recipient of Jean Sinor, Jenö Ádám, and Gunild Keetman scholarships through OAKE and AOSA. Lennie was named Teacher of the Year in 2009 for the Aberdeen Catholic Schools and currently serves as President for Sioux Valley Orff.

Diana Hawley Larsen teaches Kindergarten through sixth grade music and directs a before-school ensemble program of 60 4th, 5th and 6th graders at Norman Borlaug Elementary, a diverse public school of 375 students in the Iowa City Community School District. She holds a

B.A. in Music and Sociology/Anthropology from St. Olaf College and an M.A. in Education from the University of St. Thomas. Before moving to Iowa, she taught in St. Paul, MN and at International School Bangkok in Thailand. In 2014, prior to her 15th year of teaching children, Diana received a Barbara Potter Scholarship from the American Orff-Schulwerk Association to attend the International Summer Course at the Orff Institute in Salzburg, Austria.

Shelly Smith has been teaching general music for 24 years. She received her B.M. and M.M. degrees from the University of Nebraska-Lincoln. Shelly currently teaches children in grades Pre K-5 at Sandoz Elementary School in Omaha, Nebraska. Sandoz is a full Title I School and English Language Learner magnet site that serves 375 students. There are over 12 languages spoken by students at her school. Shelly has served as an instructor in movement and recorder for several Orff-Schulwerk teacher education courses. She is an active workshop clinician and has made numerous presentations for the Nebraska Music Educators Association. Locally, Shelly served on the board of the Great Plains Orff Chapter for 21 years.

Introduction

Artful–Playful–Mindful in Action: Orff-Schulwerk Classroom Projects for a New Generation of Learners brings to life the framework for music learning proposed by Jane Frazee in *Artful–Playful–Mindful: A New Orff-Schulwerk Curriculum for Music Making and Music Thinking*. More a collection of short stories than a reference, our new book tells the tales of music teachers across the country trying something new in their classrooms: designing three-week projects focused on either a specific rhythm or pitch concept. The first week begins with students experiencing an *Artful* model—a singing game, a folk dance, an instrumental piece that highlights a new rhythm or melody pattern. This sets the stage for a *Playful* creative task during week two, typically an improvisation or composition that allows the children to work with the musical material from week one. In the final *Mindful* week, "students show and tell us what they know and what they can do."[1] As a companion to *Artful–Playful–Mindful (APM)*, this book makes visible an Orff-inspired approach to teaching music that equally emphasizes 1) making music, 2) making up music, and 3) making sense of music.

This compilation of collaborative work produced by a group of Orff practitioners from California, Iowa, Nebraska, and South Dakota, *APM in Action* consists of 12 projects we developed and tried out with our students. In addition to the lessons, each teacher-developer shares insights and ideas as he or she reflects on how the process played out with the children.

All of us are busy, full-time teachers living in four different states, so we worked together via e-mail, Facebook, Skype, Dropbox, YouTube, and Google Drive, meeting in person from time to time in duets and trios to develop lessons, discuss successes and setbacks, and to strategize for future projects. *Just as Orff-Schulwerk was birthed as collaboration between Orff and Keetman, this book is a collaboration between teachers that brainstormed, crafted, and critiqued one another's work.* In our conversations we asked questions:

- Is it possible to help our students grow as musicians while also developing critical thinking and social skills that transfer outside the classroom?
- Which songs and pieces do you think make the best musical models?
- Which creative tasks do you find manageable for students to complete in one week's time?
- Did that mindful activity really assess what my students understood about the concept?
- How can we document and share our work with children?

As you read on, you will see the rewards we have reaped in seeking answers to these questions. We encourage readers to peruse *Artful–Playful–Mindful in Action* with *Artful–Playful–*

Mindful nearby, as the second book lays out the framework and philosophy, and the first will give you a feel for how it works with kids.

Is Orff–Schulwerk reaching our new generation of learners?

If you have picked up this book, it's likely you already know about the benefits of the Orff approach in the contemporary American elementary music classroom. You've seen children engage as active musicians, learning music by doing music. You've observed how exploring material through different media (singing, speaking, moving and playing instruments) allows children to discover the connections between music and movement. You've noticed how careful process teaching brings even students with little music background into creative improvisation and composition tasks. In this naturally differentiated learning environment, all students contribute to the musical community.

So, with all of those positive characteristics of Orff-Schulwerk, why did Jane Frazee propose a new framework for teaching music in today's classrooms? And, more specifically for this book, how have we used *APM*'s Project Model with our students?

Like most of you, we teach in real-world settings. We have become skillful at working with large, diverse classes, and the time we have with our students isn't enough to get it all done. With classes back-to-back all day, and with little time to prepare or collaborate, we were receptive to a vision that would allow us to make the most of our busy schedules. The Project Model blends the beauty of Orff-Schulwerk with the efficiency required in a public school setting.

Second, we find that *APM* allows us to marry the best of Orff-Schulwerk with what educational research considers best practice. *APM* helps us plan our instructional time wisely, prioritizing response and analysis of our students' artful and playful work over performance. And at the same time, we support the development of our students' critical thinking and metacognitive skills. *We think of* APM *as an expanded vision of* Orff-Schulwerk, *retooled for our new generation of learners.*

What are the specifics of the Project Model?

Frazee describes the Project Model as "three one-week packages beginning with performing, followed by inventing, and, lastly, thinking about musical ideas… In short, we start with an artful model, we play with it, and then we think about what we've learned."[2] Each three-week project is centered on one specific rhythm or pitch concept. Lessons in form, texture, timbre and expression unfold authentically during each project. You will see how these projects unfold with children in the coming pages.

How is this different from the traditional Orff–Schulwerk instructional model?
Orff Process in the APM *Classroom*

Process teaching is an essential contribution to Orff-inspired instruction. Master teachers may appear flowing and seamless in their instruction, yet there is structure in every successful Orff-Schulwerk lesson; flexibility and spontaneity come from learning to play with certain rules within a given form. On the AOSA website, we hear that students in an Orff classroom "start with something they know and move it into a new arena," and that "skillful questioning from teachers challenges them to explore a bit more." [3] Steven Calantropio writes that the Orff process "begins with a simple idea, builds one idea upon another, and spirals out and around the original idea to create an expanding set of perceptions." [4] Yes! Now, how do we make sure our students understand what they are experiencing? How can we get students talking about these perceptions?

Orff Media in the APM Classroom

There's room for all Orff media in *APM*, but not all in every project. *APM* challenges teachers to view Orff media as tools to be utilized only when their use will build understanding of the conceptual focus. Purposeful selection of media means not using every tool in the toolbox in every lesson. Just like a skillful woodworker uses only the tools she needs to build a chair that is both beautiful and structurally sound, so does the Orff practitioner select just the right singing game, xylophone piece, body percussion pattern, or dance that will help illuminate a musical concept for a student. Instead of taking up so much time exploring concepts in every way, *APM* reallocates that time toward the development of thinking skills and understanding of each task.

Making Sense of Mindfulness

Perhaps the characteristic that most defines *APM* is the focus on mindful work. In the project model we embrace the Orff process that works so well with our students, but extend the model to include a period dedicated to purposeful reflection. Frazee suggests, "it is primarily in the mindful stage that matters of understanding, hearing and reflective responses to past work are developed." [5]

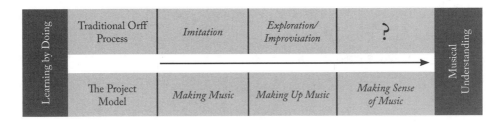

So, what does this look like? Reflective tasks typically include pairing a higher-level thinking skill with the pitch or rhythm concept:
- Students *analyze* the form or melodic contour of each others' compositions
- Students *compare and contrast* a new rhythm with a familiar one
- Students *share their perspective or ideas* about their learning during a project

I already do these types of tasks in my work with students. Why should I consider APM? If you have a system that works for you and your students, wonderful! The purpose of *APM* is to help music teachers apply a new lesson design for their bustling, multi-faceted classrooms, places where lessons typically branch out in so many directions we lose our focus. Performing and creating music with children can be so joyful, we sometimes forget to stop and give our students 1) language to talk about what they're doing, 2) opportunities to apply their understanding in different contexts, and 3) the chance to talk about how they came to make sense of a new concept.

But aren't my students demonstrating understanding through performance?

APM helps teachers focus their instructional time on developing musical understanding, not just technique. Performing demonstrates proficiency of a skill; musicianship demonstrates deeper understanding and mastery.

In *Orff-Schulwerk Today*, Frazee reminds us that:

> Learning by doing is clearly the most sensible approach to music study. Doing, however, does not guarantee understanding because it is generally preoccupied with proficiency. In other words, while Nathan may be an adept xylophone player, he may have no idea of the interplay of elements at work in the piece that he is learning. [6]

We cannot assume that our goals have been met unless we provide time for student responses. As Frazee states, "when students reflect on the music that they have made, they begin to discover the substance of the subject as well as to practice learning skills that are critical to learning in other disciplines and in everyday life." [7]

How We Applied the APM *Model in our Classrooms*

It is one thing to read a book about *APM* and something completely different to make it a part of your classroom practice. Each of the projects we have included in this book consist of two parts: 1) three sequential lessons based on a rhythmic or melodic concept, and 2) a reflection on the project from the perspective of the lesson developer. These observations address how the lesson was created, why a musical selection was made, what outcomes were chosen for assessment, how the projects worked with the students, and what we learned that would serve us in developing future *APM* projects. This type of teacher reflection is noticeably absent from other publications, but is crucial in showing how the project model works with real kids in the real world. We hope these lessons will come to life for our readers as we tried to write about the students and their learning as much as—or more than—the plan itself.

Personal Growth as Educators

The work that we have done in this book has been for our students and their learning, but putting *APM* into practice has made all of us more responsive teachers. We felt called to search through our song collections to find just the right artful piece that highlighted a rhythm or melodic concept; we brainstormed strategies for creating playful experiences that students could make their own; and we stretched ourselves to create culminating activities that would allow our students to show evidence of their musical growth and learning. We worked with colleagues with different strengths and perspectives, pulling in new ideas throughout the process. Because we did it as a team, we learned from each other while enjoying the ride.

At some point in our work together we made a realization: our interaction with *APM* resembles the project model. First, we read, discussed and explored *APM* (an artful model) with our learning community. Then we played with the model as we designed lessons for our classrooms. And now we finally make sense of our learning as we frame our understanding in this book to share with other music teachers.

Looking Ahead

We hope that the projects we share in *Artful–Playful–Mindful in Action* will inspire you to give *APM* a try in your work with children. These lessons are not intended to be rigid scripts to follow, but rather a starting point. We take you by the hand into our own classrooms, explaining how we worked through the lessons, sharing examples of student work and reflecting on how powerful *APM* has become for our professional practice. We encourage you to try out the projects we share, adapting as needed for your own unique situation, or to take over the reins and start from scratch. Consider creating your own professional learning community as you explore new possibilities together; dig in as a team! We hope you will experience how *APM* transforms an elementary music room into a hub of music making and music thinking. We wish you the best as you begin this work!

—Leonard Davis and Diana Hawley Larsen

Part 1: Rhythm Projects

Rhythm is one of the most powerful pleasures, and when we feel a pleasurable rhythm we hope it will continue. When it does, it grows sweeter.

—Mary Oliver
A Poetry Handbook